Prayers & Praises

TO OUR ALMIGHTY GOD

*Getting a Better Understanding
of Bible Verses*

BY KAREN LIVINGSTON

TATE PUBLISHING & *Enterprises*

Published by Tate Publishing & Enterprises, LLC
127 E. Trade Center Terrace | Mustang, Oklahoma 73064 USA
1.888.361.9473 | www.tatepublishing.com

Tate Publishing is committed to excellence in the publishing industry. The company reflects the philosophy established by the founders, based on Psalm 68:11,
"The Lord gave the word and great was the company of those who published it."

Book design copyright © 2008 by Tate Publishing, LLC. All rights reserved.
Cover design by Janae J. Glass
Interior design by Jacob Crissup

Published in the United States of America

ISBN: 978-1-60604-481-0
1. General Interest: Literature & Arts: Poetry
2. Christian Living: Spiritual Growth: General (poetry)
08.07.07

Prayers & Praises

TO OUR ALMIGHTY GOD

The Lord is my light and my salvation; whom shall I fear?

Psalm 27:1

Lord,
You are my light
That guides me on the right path.

There are two ways
I can go.
I can follow the light down the path of
Righteousness and eternal life.

I can stray off
To the path of darkness
Where there is pain and suffering.

If I stray,
I know you will always be there to
Guide me back to the right path.

Lord,
You loved the world so much
That you sent your son, Jesus Christ,
To suffer in pain on the cross
For the world's sins,
So the world can be right with you again,
So we can have eternal life after death.

Lord,
We fear you because
One day we will have to face your judgment,
When our life on Earth perishes.

Trust in the Lord with all thine heart; and lean not unto thine own understanding.

Proverbs 3:5

Lord,
You know my
Weaknesses and my struggles.

One of them being trust.
I know now that I have to seek you,
Ask you for guidance,
For we are not strong enough alone
To handle hardships that come our way.

Without you
We are weak.
Only through you
We are strong enough to conquer anything
That comes our way in life.

And all things, whatsoever ye shall ask in prayer, believing, ye shall receive.

Matthew 21:22

Lord,
You know my needs
If I need your help,
I need to ask in prayer.

Prayer
Is a powerful thing
To have.

If I don't ask
You won't help.

A prayer
Can be answered
The day it was prayed.

A prayer
Can be answered
In the week it was prayed.

A prayer
Can be answered in the month

That it was prayed.

A prayer
Can be answered years
After it was prayed.

God,
You hear all prayers.

Thou shalt worship the Lord thy God, and him only shalt thou serve.

Lord,
You're the only God
That we should be worshiping
Anything else is just wrong.

If we are worshiping
Other things
We are not obeying.

We would be
Sinning against you
Heavenly Father.

We should
Surrender ourselves to you, Lord,
Serving you daily.

I can do all things through Christ which strengtheneth me.

Lord,
Without your son, Jesus Christ,
We won't measure up to anything.

We are weak
Without Him in our
Hearts and souls.

Without Christ,
We wouldn't have a relationship
A time of worship with you.

Without your son, Christ,
All you see is
Our dirty hearts filled with sin.

Through your son,
Christ,
We are right with you again.

And forgive us our debts, as we forgive our debtors.

Matthew 6:12

Lord,
No matter what
We do against you
You always forgive us.

But
We have to ask your forgiveness
In order to receive forgiveness.

As you have forgiven us,
We should do the same
To the people who
Have done wrong against us.

Because
We are all the same,
We are all sinners in your eyes,
We would like to be forgiven
If we do wrong.
So we should do the same to others
Who do wrong against us.

But without faith it is impossible to please him: for he that cometh to God must believe that he is, and that he is a rewarder of them that diligently seek him.

Hebrews 11:6

Lord,
In order
To have a relationship with you,
Have faith in you,
We have to believe you exist.

We have to believe
You're the one and only God.
If we don't,
We are sinning against you.

When we talk to you,
We have to believe that you are God.

Without belief,
We don't have a relationship with you.

Follow peace with all men, and holiness, without which no
man shall see the Lord...

Hebrews 12:14

Lord,
We need to make peace
With our enemies;
Because if we don't,
We really don't know you.

If we don't make peace with people,
You will convict us
Until we make things right.

Without peace,
We can't be holy for you.

We have this burden on our heart,
For which we have to ask forgiveness from you,
In order to be holy again,
In your eyes.

Your holiness is what cleanses us
From our sin,
Only through you can we be holy.

I will never leave thee, nor forsake thee.

Hebrews 13:5

Lord,
I know you are always there
If anyone were to call upon your name
For guidance.

You are always there
Willing to help us
Even when we don't obey you
The way we should.

You are always there
Even when we stray.

You are always there
When we find our way back.

You would never leave us
Because your love for us is everlasting.

PRAYERS & PRAISES

And, Thou, Lord, in the beginning hast laid the foundation
of the earth; and the heavens are the works of thine hands...

Hebrews 1:10

Lord,
Without you
There wouldn't be life.

There wouldn't be
Such an inspirational place
For us to live.

Where we could see the beauty
Of your creations.

Like the spring when
Everything comes out of hibernation
And starts to bloom.

Without you,
There wouldn't be a place to go to
Called Heaven.

Where
We spend eternal life
With you and the angels.

Have not I commanded thee? Be strong and of a good courage; be not afraid, neither be thou dismayed: for the Lord thy God is with thee whithersoever thou goest.

Joshua 1:9

We shouldn't
Act on our feelings
But have faith that whatever
Comes our way,
Good or bad, everything will be all right.

Like the heroes we remember today
Who risked their lives to save the lives of others.

We remember
The lives that were taken that day
In that horrible tragedy.
Also their courage and the sacrifices they made
To help the people in need.

They will always be remembered as
The heroes of September 11
For their courage and bravery.

Like we remember your son,

Jesus Christ,

How He sacrificed His life for our sins.

Blessed are they which do hunger and thirst after righteousness: for they shall be filled.

Matthew 5:6

The Lord
Blesses us in many ways.

If we hunger and thirst
For His Word.
He will give us the answers
We are searching for.

If we pray to the Lord,
He will surely answer us.

If we spend time with the Lord,
He will bless us daily.

Thy word have I hid in mine heart, that I might not sin against thee.

Psalm 119:11

When we read the Word of God,
We should absorb what we read
With our mind, body, and soul.

If we have the Word of God
In our hearts,
We make the effort not to sin against
Our Heavenly Father.

Since we are human,
We make mistakes.
Our Heavenly Father will always forgive us
Of our wrongdoings because
He loves us.

Let not your heart be troubled: ye believe in God, believe also in me.

John 14:1

Lord,
You know the troubles of
My heart.

Whether
I say it or not.

Lord,
You have faith in us because
We have faith in you.

Lord,
I need your help
To get through
My troubled heart.

Lord,
I need your help
To build my trust in you.

Lord,
I need your help
To seek you instead of
Handling my pain alone.
In a way that would not glorify you.

Unto thee, O Lord, do I lift up my soul.

Psalm 25:1

Lord, you know my soul
Since you created my soul.

In order
To be cleansed from sin,
I have to surrender my soul to you.

My soul,
Has belonged to you
Since the day Jesus
Came into my heart.

My soul is yours,
Put it to good use.

Finally, brethren, whatsoever things are true, whatsoever things are honest, whatsoever things are just, whatsoever things are pure, whatsoever things are lovely, whatsoever things are of good report; if there be any virtue, and if there be any praise, think on these things.

Philippians 4:8

Lord,
The only thing that is true
Is your Word;
Any other way is done by evil.

Lord,
Anything noble we do,
We should do it for you.

Lord,
We should be just like your Son,
Jesus Christ,
Do what is right no matter
What our flesh wants.

Lord,
Everything I do should be pure,
Every thought I think,
Everything that I do throughout the day,

What I say to others,
Should be pure to your ears.

For God is my witness, whom I serve with my spirit in the gospel of his Son, that without ceasing I make mention of you always in my prayers...

Romans 1:9

Lord,
You see all.
You witness everything that goes on
In our lives, good or bad.

Lord,
Since Christ, your Son,
Came into my heart and soul,
I should share the joy I have with
The world around me.

So they can have the joy I feel
With my salvation that was freely given to me.

Lord,
Because of Your Son,
Christ,
We can be right with You.
So with every prayer we mention You,
To thank You for everything that You do for us.

And herein do I exercise myself, to have always a conscience void of offense toward God, and toward men.

Acts 24:16

Lord,
You know my conscience,
You know what I struggle with.

You know my heart,
Whom I have offended and been offended by
Even if it's not clear to me,
Who and why.

Lord,
Help me clear my conscience,
So I can clear my mind.

Casting down imaginations, and every high thing that exalt-eth itself against the knowledge of God, and bringing into captivity every thought to the obedience of Christ...

2 Corinthians 10:5

Lord,
You know every thought
I think.

You know
Every emotion I feel,
Good or bad.

Any negative thought
I have against myself
Is a sin against You.

Anything positive
I think about myself
Is glorifying You.

Lord,
Please help me
Get ungodly thoughts
Out of my mind.

Lord,
Please help me
Get ungodly feelings out of my heart,
So I can feel free and joyful in Your presence.

So I can glorify You
With all my heart.

For if ye forgive men their trespasses, your heavenly Father will also forgive you...

Matthew 6:14

Lord,
Please help me
Forgive the people who have
Hurt me.

Sorry, God,
For I have sinned against You
In the worst way.

Sorry, God,
For my self-destructive behavior,
Past and recent.

Sorry, God,
For not having more
Faith in You.

Sorry, God,
For not putting my trust
In You like I should.

Sorry, God,
For giving in,
Giving up on life itself.

Life that You gave me
To live;
I am just throwing it away
Because of struggles I can't face
On my own.

Sorry, God,
Can You forgive me?

Gracious Heavenly Father,
I need Your help and guidance
More than anything right now.

I can't battle these
Inner demons alone.

Gracious Heavenly Father,
Help me
Face my deepest, darkest secrets.

Guide me and protect me
From any and all evil
That will come my way
On my path of self discovery.

Whether they be
Good or bad discoveries.

Gracious Heavenly Father,
Give me the strength to
Face my past
To see the future.

God is our refuge and strength, a very present help in trouble.

Psalm 46:1

God.
Please give me security
When I am at my darkest hour.

God,
Please give me courage
To face the challenges that
Await me.

God,
Please give me the strength
To get me through.

God,
Please give me safety from
What's to come whatever it may be,
Even if it's from myself.

He will not always chide: neither will he keep his anger forever.

Psalm 103:9

Lord,
I need your help
Through the darkness of the world
Around me.

Lord,
I need your help
To confront my anger.

Lord,
I need your help
To conquer the darkness of
My past.

Lord,
I need your help
As I go on my journey of
Self discovery.

How precious also are thy thoughts unto me, O God! how
great is the sum of them! If I should count them, they are
more in number than the sand: when I awake, I am still
with thee.

Psalm 139:17, 18

Heavenly Father,
When You look at me,
What do You see?

Do You see
The good in me?

Do You see
All the evil that
Suffocates my soul?

Heavenly Father,
Give me the strength
To get through the day.

Give me the wisdom
To know the difference between
Right and wrong.

Heavenly Father,
Do You see my soul shivering with fear
From the darkness of the world?

That was the true Light, which lighteth every man that comes into the world.

John 1:9

Creator of all things,
I need Your help
To understand things
I don't understand.

Creator of all things,
Help me understand
What is going on inside of me.

Creator of all things,
Help me see the good in everything
Instead of the bad.

Creator of all things,
Help me see what is behind
The fear in me.

Creator of all things,
Help me conquer evil so
I can live for Your glory.

So that we may boldly say, The Lord is my helper, and I will not fear what man shall do unto me.

Hebrews 13:6

Heavenly Father,
Give me the courage
To take off my mask that is telling the world
Everything is fine.

Heavenly Father,
Give me the knowledge of
What's really going on.

Heavenly Father,
Give me insight into
My fear.

What
Am I afraid of?

Why
Am I afraid of it?

How
Can I overcome my fears?

Why do my emotions
Come and go,
Like day and night?

What's
Really bothering me,
Deep within?

Yea, though I walk through the valley of the shadow of death,
I will fear no evil: for thou art with me; thy rod and thy staff
they comfort me.

Psalm 23:4

Heavenly Father,
Please help me
Not feel controlled by others.

Heavenly Father,
Please help me understand.

Why,
Do I continually feel,
Unsafe with myself?

I feel that
Anything around me
Could be used as a weapon
Of self-destruction.

Afraid
That my emotions will spin me
Out of control.

Afraid
One day my emotions are going to
End up killing me.

Heavenly Father,
How am I supposed to get out my emotions
Without taking out myself?

Shall vain words have an end? or what emboldeneth thee that thou answerest?

Job 16:3

O Lord of Lords,
Please help me,
For the littlest things get to me.

If I hear
A distant argument,
It will put chills through me.

The pain of
Worthlessness will come back
And that makes me sad.

O Lord of Lords,
Please help me,
For the biggest thing I fear
Is myself.

I feel like
I am my worst enemy.
I don't know
How to forgive myself for things
I have done to myself.

I feel like
I am being held prisoner
In my body and soul.

Afraid
To be alone with myself;
In fear
I might go crazy.

O Lord of Lords,
Protect me from any
And all evil
That might come my way.

Blessed are ye, when men shall revile you, and persecute you, and shall say all manner of evil against you falsely, for my sake.

Matthew 5:11

Show me the way,
And I will follow You in Your glory.

Dear God,
Please help me understand
Why I do the things I do.

Dear God,
Help me forget
What I have been told
In my past.

Dear God,
Please help me get past
The hurt that has been inflicted upon me
Year after year
Verbally and physically.

Dear God,
Please help me
Believe in myself
Not what others have said to me.

Dear God,
I believe in you
Since you believed in me first.

There shall no evil befall thee, neither shall any plague come nigh thy dwelling. For he shall give his angels charge over thee, to keep thee in all thy ways.

Psalm 91:10, 11

God,
Please help me
Understand my heavy heart.

Is there something
I have not confessed that
You want me to confess?

Why,
Am I nervous
Around groups of people?

Why,
Do I have this fear
That people are out to get me
To hurt me?

Why,
Do I have this fear
That I'm going to die in the middle
Of the night?

Dear God,
Please give me
The wisdom and strength to
Confront whatever is making my heart heavy.

So I can continue
Living life
In Your glory.

The angel of the Lord encampeth round about them that fear him, and delivereth them.

Psalm 34:7

Thank You
For this blessed wonderful day.

Where
We can start new each morning
Learning from the previous day
What not to do in the day before us.

Thank You
For the challenges
We are confronted with that
Test our faith in You.

Thank You
For sending Your Son
To die for our sins.
If it weren't for Him,
We would never get to know You.

Thank You
For caring
When nobody else did.

Thank You
For everything that You
Do for me.

Thank You
For prayers that You've answered,
Big and small.

Thank You
For being there when
I felt I had no one to turn to.

Thank You
For showing me the way
When I get lost in
The darkness of the world.

For You are my light
In this world
Full of darkness.

KAREN LIVINGSTON

Giving thanks always for all things unto God and the Father in the name of our Lord Jesus Christ...

Ephesians 5:20

Thank You
For giving me the strength to
Get through the day.

Thank You
For believing in me.

Thank You
For the challenges
I faced today.

Thank You
For the mercies
You give us every day.

Thank You
For sending Your angels to
Protect us every day.

And not only so, but we glory in tribulations also: knowing that tribulation worketh patience...

Romans 5:3

Thank You
For another blessed day.

Thank You
For the bad things
So we can enjoy the good things.

Thank You
For protecting me
Throughout the night.

Thank You
For always being there
When I needed someone to
Talk to.

Like
You forgive and forget
All sins
I commit against You,

Give me
A heart of forgiveness,
Not a heart of regret.

PRAYERS & PRAISES

53

In my distress I cried unto the Lord, and he heard me.

Psalm 120:1

Lord,
You are there when I am distressed;
You would never turn Your back on me.

When
The world turns cold,
Your light is always there to
Guide me.

When
I feel let down by the world,
Your presence lifts up my soul,
And I know I am not alone.

Just knowing You are there,
Gives me strength to
Get through anything that comes my way.

What time I am afraid, I will trust in thee.

Lord, You know
My heart,
My struggles, and my pain.

Lord, you know
When I am happy and
When I am really not.

You're always there
To help me through
Day and night.

I can come to you
For guidance
No matter what the time.

I never
Have to be afraid.

You accept me
For who I am.

KAREN LIVINGSTON

Lord,
I cry out to You
For help.

Lord,
I cry out to You
For guidance.

Lord,
I am weak without You.

Lord,
I cry out to You.
You're my strength to get through
The darkness of the world.

You are my light through
The darkness of life.

Create in me a clean heart, O God; and renew a right spirit within me.

Psalm 51:10

Lord,
Please help me purify
My heart.

Help me confess sins
That hold me back from
Knowing You.

Cleanse
My heart and soul
From all evil it holds, that
Evil won't guilt me for eternity.

Lord,
Save me from
My fleshly sin of self-destruction.

If any of you lack wisdom, let him ask of God, that giveth to all men liberally, and upbraideth not; and it shall be given him.

James 1:5

Lord,
Give me the wisdom,
To do right.

I can glorify You
Instead of giving into my fleshly sin of
Self-destruction.

Lord,
Give me the wisdom
To defeat the evil corrupting
My life.

Lord,
Give me the wisdom
To live a godly life that
Glorifies You daily.

Though he slay me, yet will I trust in him...

Job 13:15

Lord,
Please help me to
Trust in You.

To be content with
Who I am as a person.

Lord,
Please help me
See past all this pain.

Please,
Help me not to give into
Self-destruction.

Lord,
Please help me
See You are the light guiding me through
The darkness of evil.

But we will give ourselves continually to prayer, and to the ministry of the word.

Acts 6:4

We need to continually
Pray to God.

To continue a good relationship
With God.

We need to read
The Word of God daily so
He can talk with us.

The more we read the Word of God
The more we grow spiritually closer to Him.

But thou, O Lord, art a shield for me; my glory, and the lifter up of mine head.

Psalm 3:3

God is my protector
From my enemies in this world.

He is the reason I exist.
With every breath I take I will
Glorify Him.

With
Every step I take,

With
Every word I speak,

He will be shown in
Everything I do.

My voice shalt thou hear in the morning, O Lord; in the
morning will I direct my prayer unto thee, and will look up.

Psalm 5:3

God,
You are there for me
Every day.

You listen to my
Concerns and worries.

You listen to my
Praises.

You are there for me
Day after day.

Through
The good times,

Through
The bad times,

You are there for me always.
That alone
Fills me with joy.

This poor man cried, and the Lord heard him, and saved him out of all his troubles.

Psalm 34:6

God,
You are there to
Protect me
From the evil in the world.

Through You,
I can accomplish anything.

In anything I do,
You will be glorified.

When I am at a loss,
I look to You
to get strength to go on.

When I am afraid,
I look to You
For the courage to go on.

God,
Through You,
I am capable of
Anything and everything.

I will both lay me down in peace, and sleep: for thou, Lord, only makest me dwell in safety.

Psalm 4:8

God,
Knowing You are there,
Watching over me,
Brings me peace of mind.

Knowing
You are there
Is comfort to me.

Knowing
You are in control of all things
Brings comfort to my soul.

Knowing
I can cast my concerns and cares
To you
Brings comfort to my soul.

Knowing
That I am not alone in the journey of life
Brings me comfort and peace
Within my soul.

For the Lord is great, and greatly to be praised: he is to be
feared above all gods.

Psalm 96:4

God,
You are a wonderful God
For all the things
You do.

No matter
If I am going through a storm,
If the waters are calm,
I will praise You in everything
I do.

I will praise You
In the midst of a storm.
There is a reason for all things
That happen.

The times of trials are
What make me a stronger person;
To help others going through the same things.

If it weren't for the turbulence
In my life,
I wouldn't be able to appreciate the glorious times
In my life spent with You.

I will praise Thee through
My journey in life.

Through You,
Anything is possible.

Let the saints be joyful in glory: let them sing aloud upon their beds.

Psalm 149:5

No matter
What is happening in my life,
I know I can always rejoice
In Your presence.

Even though
I don't understand
Why things happen the way they do,
I should rejoice in Your glory.

Knowing
You have a reason
Behind everything You do,
And all is for good.

I rejoice
In Your glory always.

Great is our Lord, and of great power: his understanding is
infinite.

Psalm 147:5

God,
You are an almighty God.

Nothing
Is impossible for You
To handle.

Through You,
There is nothing impossible
For me to handle.

You can
Change people's hearts
To do right.

You can make
Impossible things possible.

Through You,
Anything is possible.

You have the power to
Change the world.

Through You,
We can change the world,
One soul at a time.

I sought the Lord, and he heard me, and delivered me from all my fears.

Psalm 34:4

God,
You are there always.

You are always faithful
When we as humans slip into
The world of sin pushing You away.

When
We need you the most,
You are there.

You know all,
You see all.

No prayer
Is too hard for You
To answer.

You know what is best
And supply the needs of the world.

I can come to You for anything.
You will never let me down.
We as humans will always let You down.

Your mercies are so wonderful,
That You will always forgive us for
Abandoning You.

As long as we come to You
In prayer,
You will forgive us of
Our wrongdoings.

KAREN LIVINGSTON